Explanatory Value

Explanatory Value

Poems by

Florence Fogelin

Cover design by Shay Culligan
Cover photograph, "Seattle Harbor" by Rosamond Orford

ISBN: 978-1-954353-55-8

Kelsay Books
502 South 1040 East, A-119
American Fork, Utah, 84003

for
Eric, John, and Lars

And
Bob

Explanatory value is a technical philosophical term. When a variable isn't independent for certain, it's an explanatory variable. In a world of limitless questions and answers, explanations offer value, or fail to do so.

Some questions don't warrant a question mark.
—Anne Carson

Acknowledgments

Grateful acknowledgment is made to the editors of the journals and anthologies who first published the following poems. The poems, sometimes in earlier versions, appeared as follows:

Birchsong: Poetry Centered in Vermont, vol. II: "Spring Cleaning"
Facing the Light (Redgreene Press, 2001): "A Voice from the Edge of the Sea," "Balance Scale" (with another title), "Black Hole," "Communion" (another title), "Facing the Light"
Porter Gulch Review: "The Realm of Happily-Ever-After," "Likenesses"
Prairie Schooner: "Living Memory," "Someday Give a Day"
Roads Taken: Contemporary Vermont Poetry: "Orthophony: Reading"

Contents

Part III

Part I

The Year We Didn't Go to China...

We didn't teach
our language or our ways,
Western thought, the Socratic method,
skepticism, philosophy.

We didn't learn
—as we were told—
to represent in all we did
the United States of America.

We didn't get to know
whether to trust our *woban,*
who'd know everything we did
and help us do it.

We didn't do them any harm,
the ones we would have come to love,
who'd understand—but nervously—
why we had come.

The year we didn't go to China
we didn't foresee
Tiananmen, a year in the future,
where death surely would have taken
the friends we didn't make.

We didn't go;
perhaps we saved their lives.
Fulbrightless we went instead to Italy.
Clean hands. Why do I feel guilty.

Balance Scale

Form ever follows function.
 —Louis Sullivan

Idle—gathering dust—
no longer oiled or polished—
no longer used—it's tossed—
or saved—simply to rust.

Function's first to go—
What's left—are beauty's bones.
A rug beater disarms
the line between force and show.

The brass balance scale
quivers—while it waits—
But time appreciates
its shaped material—

design—color—mass—
its inlaid marble base,
lustrous scoops and trays
useless—and meant to last.

In Living Memory

I'm trying to remember you
among smiling photographs,
trying to remember verbs
but left with nouns,
snapshots of memory.

I'm trying to remember the day
we agreed had been somehow *perfect,*
spent walking a country road
while the windshield was being repaired,
and we tried—
we even had a Guide to Wildflowers—
to identify goldenrod.
Who knew there were so many kinds?
Who but you would understand
our appointment with a summer day?
And share the reference to Santayana?

Strength in Small Numbers

for Giorgio Morandi

Bottles and jars are safe
subjects in a troubled, fascist time:
faceless, safe
to arrange at will,
to place together or apart, safe

simply being what they are:
one, another one,
containers without contents,
content to be no more
than what they seem.

Explanatory Value: Language

Because there is no end to information given,
we claim we understand, data-driven
to make inferences to the best explanation,
and put the horizon where we please.

We are adept at language—
as much a part of us as our DNA—
and navigate worlds with words,
arguments with ourselves and each other:
>   *Although I did it, in spite of myself and what you*
>   *may think, notwithstanding what they say and not*
>   *to mention my age, in point of fact as a first approximation*
>   *let's say that...*

We are enmeshed in a world of facts
and the machinery of language—
Don't blame the words; they oil our gears,
enable us to think and appreciate nonsense
and are themselves our joy, our bane, and our salvation.

Orthophony: Reading

Orthophony: William Russell,
39th edition, 1871

That poetry should come to this!
Garrison Keillor celebrating love in mid-July,
a lugubrious monotone:
Shall I compare thee to a summer's day...
Shakespeare's words with a sad-sack poet's voice.

Reading aloud was schooled:
public speaking, speech, elocution...orthophony.
> *Persons who commence practice with a feeble utterance
> can attain the full command of clear, forcible, and varied
> tone.*
Russell wrote—and teachers taught—with examples
from Shakespeare, Bryant, Mrs. Hemans, Milton:
pitch...stress...force...melody...whispering...
even half-whispering...

You see a page of poetry,
but can you listen to it? Say it? Synch your lips with it?
Let the poem tell you where to breathe.
Practice breathing.

What Difference Does It Make

Each afternoon at 4 p.m. I sip a cup of tea,
listen to the woes of the world and doze,
awakening to more of the same.
Or different. Different names…
What difference does it make to me,
comfortable, financially secure, warm.
Still, I listen,
go to the kitchen and help myself
to a glass of wine.

I listen, barely listen
to the soothing voices—NPR,
not like those on cable news—
go back to the kitchen for cheese-and-crackers
and pour myself another wine.

I've lived in troubled times—
who hasn't?—but I was blessed
throughout the 20th century:
father, husband, sons
slalomed past the gates of war,
never got or gave a shot.
Coffee, tea, and wine soothe my days,
listening to the 21st:
the world is mad; the world is melting.

The Realm of Happily-Ever-After

Once I telephoned a dead man,
a housepainter recommended by a friend.
His widow said she didn't mind my call;
she talked so freely I could only listen.
He was kind, he was nice; she longed for him
every day. She paused. *And in the night.*
She thanked me for listening,
not knowing that my days and nights
had taken on new meaning

as I returned to cleaning house
and putting toys away,
to *When is Daddy coming home?*
ironing his shirts, inhaling
the steam's faint smell of sweat,
wrapping myself in their XL sleeves.

Explanatory Value: Naming

for Primo Levi

We talk comfortably about
      crib death syndrome
      clinical depression   ephemera
      irregularities   anomalies   obsession
      evil

and leave the subject
to those who will go on and on—
scientists, philosophers, survivors—
trying to explain beyond naming
the rock on which our ship shatters.

Likenesses

A smile is hard to hold
for the slow-exposure shutter speed
of a nineteenth-century camera,

so they look serious and severe being captured,
posed as versions of themselves:
farmers, wives, widows, children
staring across time at nobody in particular.

I like to hold them in my hands,
whether they liked their likenesses or not:
tintype icons, their faces, eyes, expressions
more real because they are strangers.

Help

Jessie Williams, retired after years of cleaning
at the home of the company president,
was proudly receiving a monthly check
from the government. She called;
she wanted to visit my mother,
Just to say Thank You.

My mother had set up her maid
with Social Security when it was new,
helped with papers and payment,
urged her to get it everywhere else she went.
I did, and I made sure that others joined, too.

They sat together on the living room sofa,
sharing old times and the doings of children
with soft Virginia accents.
1960.
Two women. One white. One black.

I joined them at the dining room table
for tea and cake with silver spoons and teacups
I now proudly call my own, remembering
when neighbors sometimes called my parents
niggerlovers.

Explanatory Value: Answers

A heron leaves the lake to land
in a fresh-mown olive grove,
answering a need that I don't understand,
knowing what I do of heron-food and heron-love.

***

The sea colors itself according to its needs
and those of changing light and air.
My questions are as ill-formed as storm clouds,
the answers raining everywhere.

***

Cairns inform our climbs;
a roadcut opens a geology book:
signs of evolution, time's slow hands.
Nature's hard at work, silently explaining.

Nails

The old rocking chair sits askew
on the tilted porch with its rotting wood
held together with rusting nails.
A derelict farmhouse,
windows boarded up so racoons can't get in
and damage—what?—
mattresses, boots and dresses, vegetable peelers.

Home to a hardworking farmer and his hardworking wife,
a barn full of cows, trees full of sap, hives with bees.
It wasn't idyllic though the view of the lake is lovely.
Quarantined by daily chores,
isolated, lonely, even with children—
one of whom lives down the road in a trailer.

They nailed a life together.
The radio was all they had
to hear what they were missing.
Hired help helped, children washed dishes
and called in the cows from pasture,
the doctor came on house calls.
Going to town was a treat,
Sunday church a weekly looking-forward-to,
choir practice, a quilting bee,
a roof-raising followed by a potluck supper.
Now it's a derelict farmhouse
held together with rusty nails and memories.
I remember.

A Long Day

Morning
      Noon
            Afternoon
                  Evening
                        Night
in a death-empty house.
Mourning is like a trick candle:
blown out, it pops alight again.

I watch the second hand tick patiently around the dial
to accomplish just a minute.

Orthophony: Listening

The chief characteristics of utterance are properties equivalent to those which are comprehended in music.
                    Orthophony: William Russell, 39th edition, 1871

My mother's gold bracelet
clasps my wrist, a gift
when I was born from her voice teacher,
who'd wanted her to study in New York.

Closing the door to spare us
what she called her *noise,*
she practiced endless scales…
inhaling…song fragments…*sostenuto*…
concentrating not on words, but vowels.
I was proud that I heard her calling me
down at the riverbank, two blocks away.
Lehar's local *Merry Widow.*
No one else's mother was as pretty.

Without the glamour of an aria,
I work on recitative, trying to make music
with italics and line breaks, envying notation:
crescendo, rests, repeats, dynamics—*pp*—*ff*—
mouthing words *sotto voce,*
my utterance soft and personal
as something thin and gold.

Part II

You Come by Registered Mail

I've slept with you for decades,
so I could put you under the bed.
Or in the attic.
An urn to decorate the sideboard.
Perhaps in the lake, I said.
You said, *That's disgusting.*

I sleep with a pillow at my back
deeply from midnight to 4 a.m.
By late afternoon I'm home and done
doing things that seem to make me normal.
I did what you said
and threw the paltry dust of you in the dumpster.
That's not tonight what leaves me hollowed out;
it's eating alone by candlelight.

Touchstones

Look, look what I found—the #1 rock!
I teased my son—*Go look for #2—*
but lost my favorite years ago in moving:
round, glacier-tumbled,
salt & pepper, sized-to-hand,
with one black stroke.

Rocks speak to me, seek me out,
tell me that I need to ask better questions:
answers conglomerate, embedded
by time and pressure, heat and cold.
On windowsills and bookshelves,
my pebbles and rocks come from everywhere I've been.
Some are lost, some are found.
If I cracked them open
what would be their stories.

Collage

A juxtaposition
of this'n'that,
a composite,
hodge-podge,
conglomerate,
agglomerate,
pastiche.

Montage,
a blend,
mixture,
admixture,
a rag-bag,
salmagundi,
a callimaufry.

Bricolage,
medley,
a hash,
a potpourri,
an assemblage,
aggregate,
jumble,

Mélange,
an olio,
mish-mash,
a combination,
amalgram,
an omnium-gatherum.
A mess.

Material Culture

I envy her Jackson-Pollocked floor,
her studio's clutter and oily smells.
Backstage—that tangle of wires and gels,
magical stuff from a hardware store.

No wonder they cherish voluptuous cellos,
bouquets of brushes, pink satin toe shoes,
canvas, marble, cameras, and tutus.
With loving care they rosin their bows.

Palettes of words: I envision a keyboard
of synonyms, a tool chest of lyrics,
poetry drawn with pastel sticks,
my sheet of paper vividly metaphored.

I write and erase, confide and cancel.
Always a soloist, all on my own,
lonely, restless, stripped to the bone,
with tapping feet I dance with a pencil.

We Teach Our Children How to Thank

Better to give than to receive love
particulate in tissue paper.
I rattle the box, admire the ribbon,
exaggerate the difficulty of untying the knot.
It's heavy, not too big—
His tremble slows my hands to a whisper.

This is a moment to dread:
he—that I will guess what it is;
I—that he will measure
and find wanting my appreciation.
What can I say to a face so small and so ferocious?
I wish myself a miser.

Now it's mine, *Just what I wanted:*
a shiny black teapot,
red dribbled around the rim,
as careless/careful as the pottery bowl
he'd made himself and splashed
a confident yellow.

I washed it carefully today,
re-shelved it, fingering the glaze.
I never use it anymore; a teabag's more convenient…
After all, it's the thought that counts.

Next-to-the-Greatest Generation

We invaded the school grounds from up the river bank,
spied on our neighbors, and thrilled to the slaughter
of celluloid Japs and Nazis on Saturday afternoons.
With lemon juice turned legible by candle flame,
we kept count of tanks and jeeps on flatcars
groaning toward the docks, then waved goodbye
to ships that disappeared one night,
the fleet aimed, we'd learn, for Normandy.

Courageously swinging our demographics
through childhood and down a century,
we marched fearlessly against war,
wearing our peace-signs like medals.

Another June, with lingering bravado,
we cycled past shifting Norman sandbars.
Fat, drooling cows were still knee-deep in grass,
the apple trees again in flower.
Cemetery flags snapped to signal friend or foe:
German. French. American. No one we knew.
Like gourmet cats we lapped crème fraîche
and washed our mouths with calvados.

Orthophony: Writing

*Poetry is vocal, but it should claim the right
to make an interesting remark.*
                                    —Robert Pinsky

I mean my poetry to last beyond
the vapor trail that is my breath:
words—the chosen ones—
written for sense and sound.

Poems read are music to the mind and to the ear,
but they can live on the page, waiting for you
to listen, to breathe them into life
and tell you what to hear.

Performance doesn't make them true,
a whisper make them secret.
This is a soundless poetry reading—
word-for-word, music written just for you.

A Letter to Robert Frost

for Seamus Heaney, 1939–2013

I went to Franconia recently
and sat on your porch, wishing we could talk
about the late Seamus Heaney who,
but for age, could have been your friend.
An Irishman. Like you, a classicist.

Years ago I lunched with him in a Vermont farmhouse
much like yours—old and small, with walls awry,
and doors that wouldn't close.
Words and cadences poured from him
as freely as the wine we drank, laughing together
before he talked, soberly, to a crowded college room.
Then he won the Nobel Prize.

I heard his interview on BBC
for Pick Your Favorite Poem Day.
Asked for his, Heaney didn't really want to say.
Forced, *Well, the* Iliad,
a choice that…*wouldn't do. We mean—in English.*
[pause]
Stopping by Woods on a Snowy Evening.
[dead air]
Robert Frost.
[dead air]
Who?
An American… no longer living…

You and Heaney walked on dirt,
your poems rooted in the soil of speech,
not in a hothouse of rich vocabulary:
The very 'there-you-are-and-where-are-you?'
of poetry itself, said Heaney.

Wherever you are, I hope you've welcomed him, ·
invited him for dinner, shared words and whiskey.
To love poetry is to study it, you said.
I see you as neighbors, elbows on the kitchen table,
talking craft, suspicious—eyeing, testing one another
as one might test the sharpness of a knife.

Starvation

Some admired the slowness of her death,
made of it a *human testimony.*
The doctor's tubes sustained my mother's breath;
his ex-wife appreciated the alimony.

Meanwhile Irish patriots, starving for their cause,
perished with prolonged publicity:
young men who died to challenge laws,
exploiting the uses of their mortality.

Health care's the vital sign of our society;
we live for others and may not die alone.
Long life becomes a gainful industry—
kindness for dogs, not for our own.

Minor Planet #2181

How would you like the world to end?
Asteroids regularly make the news—
Hollywood often makes it apocalyptic.
I'd like to hear something—anything—
about Minor Planet #2181,
glad for the recognition.

Asteroid Fogelin, named for my son,
is small, but it could make an impact,
give this world a much-needed kick in the pants—
smash-up retribution
for our fouling of the planet.

As If It Matters

In Heaven you will meet again.
She's in a better place.
God wanted her to be with him.
There is a reason for everything.

September 11, 2001.
Ask does it matter
that she's your wife,
one,
or one of thousands, victim
of war, plague, accident, murder, illness?
Does it matter
how old, how many children,
the job, the usual obituary?

Say that, like all of us,
she didn't choose to be born,
didn't ask to die.
Say she chose to be your wife,
that death is a singular event.
Speak of love. Be specific:
her smell, fresh from the bath.

Dear God:
Teach us how to grieve.
Teach us how to forgive the comforters.

Communion

This morning I enjoyed a croissant
with marmalade and two cups of coffee,
surrounded by walls of newsprint and photographs,
today's dumb show of suffering
that hid the clinks of cups and spoons,
genteel sipping.
Across the pink, freshly ironed tablecloths,
I faced the eyes of the dying,
gray multiples of hopelessness,
the patience of starvation,
a weird lack of anger.

I thought of God
and though I rarely do,
I took a sugar cube and lowered it,
cradled in a silver spoon,
and watched it stain and crumble.
I raised my cup to each woman,
her arms holding the same emaciated child,
cupped my hands around the cup
and drained it.

My Fingernails Are Clean

Showered, drying my hair in a breeze
that keeps the Tuscan afternoon
from being just a bit too warm,
I holiday among an offering
of tasseled hyacinths and poppies, orchids,
daisies, buttercups—sweet *fiori spontaneii*—
gather a bouquet and arrange it for the table.
How can I atone for this perfect, beautiful day.

One raped her, then another, and another—soldiers
laughing at her sagging breasts, lice, matted hair—
and opened her up with a knife. *Who'd think
the filthy crone would menstruate again,* they joked.
When her cries were done and she was useless
as a limp bird to a cat, they butchered what was left.
The young reporter puked who found
the fly-infested meat of her fouling a field
of buttercups and daisies, poppies, tasseled hyacinths.

Her flies are not the ones that pester me,
hers far away across the Adriatic.
The poppies are the same—each the iridescent
satin skin of a newborn child,
washed, dried, powdered. Sweet petal-flesh—
how quickly they wilt…
Some flowers are more long-lasting. Sometimes
the babe becomes a killer.

Facing the Light

Who doesn't love a snowstorm,
the beginning dance of snowflakes?
Soft white lips whisper on my old windowpanes
frosty glyphs like X-rays, death threats
manipulated by some new technology. I'm afraid
I don't understand the language of fractals. (Yes,
of course it's beautiful. What's wrong with me?)

Light isn't like this except on winter days,
when cold thins the walls against the bright surround.
Gallery lighting invades my reading room;
it seeks me even in the center hall—
kaleidoscopic shards spinning out of fields
flat with snow and filled with Greeks who train at me
their polished shields and glittering bits of mirrors.
(If surgery's required, can the patient tell them
to turn down the lights?)

When I was small, I'd time it so museum guards
wouldn't see me duck beneath the frame
to rise in the embrace of a lighthouse lens,
held within its prism rings, dizzied by
its shattered light. I'd wave my arms
to make them bleed the colors of the rainbow,
spin and twirl my terror into nausea
until I fell within the spiral of my skirt.

I was never afraid of the dark
but of the flashlight
that found me in the closet, and behind,
the bright menace of a comforting smile.

Part III

Unknown Girl on the T

She's good at it, juggling toys,
a diaper bag, stroller, two kids,
one a baby—young, too young,
black, a good chance that she's single.

(An educated guess? Racial
stereotype? What do people-watchers
make of me—so white and married-looking
I don't need my lost wedding ring.)

I marvel at her cheer and competence,
a girl-child doing well
what I found overwhelming,
twice her age and privileged.

She tells the boy to get his stuff,
fusses with his mittens,
makes a game of how they won't cooperate.
Mothering.

Mass. General…The station's
coming fast…It's not my stop,
or I would help….I'd try
to open doors….

She slips equipment and the baby
on her hip and finds a hand
to hold the boy's—but the baby
cries and spits the pacifier.

I watch her rearrange her bundles
on the platform, see her shoulders
face the challenge of the stairs,
see the pacifier—in her mouth.

Dear mothering-child,
Blessings, fare thee well.
I hope…I hope…What shall I hope.
College? A job? Equal opportunity?

I hope your kid grows up
to be a rock star or an astrophysicist,
tells the world he owes it to his mom.
I hope you win the lottery.

Explanatory Value: The World of Books

Open the book, she said, *somewhere near the middle.*
I hit the four-color bleed of a Kansas cornfield,
next, dividing half in half (flipping a page or two),
the Pacific surf and Monterey pines.
　　　　I loved the first day of school, the smell of new books,
　　　　the geography book that fired my wanderlust.
The spine's gentle crack opened
to my first view of Northern New England,
and I wanted to be there—
fall foliage pierced by white village church spires.

We took our textbooks home,
put scissors, tape, and shopping bags
on the dining room table
and made covers with corners crisp as new-made beds.

Driving north on I-91
at the cut through rocks at McIndoe Falls,
the North Country reaches ahead.
It's a view only a rucksacked hiker would have seen
when I was a grade-school child in Virginia,
longing to live in New England.
Drowned by a dam, the falls live only in name;
log runs and hill farms are tales of the past.

Geography's even slower than history;
geology slower yet.
Landscape is an open book
of slow-motion photography.

A Selfie in the Old Folks Home

O brave new world, that has such creatures in it.
—Shakespeare

It's not called that, of course:
a Continuing Care Retirement Community,
where every day you face your future
and everyone talks of the past.
Each time I open my door
I see new friends, brave smiles
supported by walkers, canes,
and physical therapy.

As best I can, I return them even though
I've always hated smiling for the birdie.
I feel I'm posing for a selfie,
new-girl conscious of my face.
Selfies don't remember cameras, their technicalities:
lenses, f-stops, depth of field,
the acceptable circle of confusion.

I'm learning to be accustomed to being here—
here where I know that I belong:
Look at me. Look at where I am.
OK, so I look serious…Just don't call me wise.

A Mind of Winter

Icicles edge a curled sheet of snow
slipping from the roof—sharks' teeth
aiming to eat the house.
Crystal twigs glisten in the sunlight;
weightless snowflakes heavying boughs of pines.

Unless you've known bitter cold,
the misery of outliving the warmth of a husband,
words cannot convey how harsh
is the cold, cold wind.

The Ears Have It

Lightbulb-changing jokes come to mind
and Cecil B. DeMille's cast of thousands.
The stage is packed, everyone hard at work
making music.

The clangor of a symphony,
a Wagner rehearsal at Carnegie Hall,
jackhammers my brain to rubble.
molto molto molto fortissimo.
How loud, O Lord, is loud enough?

Homeward bound, the subway doors open
to the tapping of a single steel pan
resonating quietly through the station,
a haunting Caribbean voice that follows me home.

Avertive Vision

Incipient glaucoma has me on edge
about the edges of my field of vision.

Each mechanical button-click
responds to a Geminid,

meteoroids I see
as if through a foggy night in December.

I try hard not to shift my eyes
away from center—better

to see in the periphery
stars I couldn't otherwise glimpse.

The doctor says I'm fine,
but come back for the Perseids.

We exchange a sideways glance.
I wonder what I'm missing.

A Voice from the Edge of the Sea

Well, if that's what it takes to be a tree,
I'll try it.
It looks like certain death,
but death is, after all, what one makes of it.
I'll cantilever from this rocky coast,
capture the morning light
and a fraction of the afternoon's.
I'll laminate my roots to the stone.
I'll find a way.

And I'll be famous:
the more I risk, the more I'm photographed.
I'll laugh at anyone who tries to pry me off this cliff.
The wind thinks whiplash is the trick…
And all that frantic foam,
its self-deluding, self-destructive rage,
wave after wave mortifying its wavy flesh.
I'll be here, here at home
until I won't, the same as you.

When you snap my picture,
frame and hang it on the wall,
you'll see the spitting image of yourself,
not nature's lucky residue:
your gnarled limbs, arthritic hands,
the proud portrait of your scars, your flaws.

Lawnoments for Sale

Yard Art.
It's a familiar wooden cut-out silhouette:
she's watering petunias with a fake watering can
to beautify a slab of grass.
Always popular: loons and frogs,
wings and legs gone wild in the wind.
In each neighborhood the Crazy House of Christmas Lights.

Yard Art.
He built it in his SoCal neighborhood—Watts Towers—
took artistic dedication to the heights in his own backyard,
almost 100 feet tall, some of them,
leaving beauty, strength, ambition, and detritus.
Then walked away.

Yard Art.
Mad King Ludwig adorned the grounds of Herrenchiemsee
with glass orbs, a long-lived craze.
Poised on a pedestal or floating in a birdbath,
mirrored and colorful to attract hummingbirds,
they're sold at Walmarts:
Gazing Balls. Only 79¢!

Explanatory Value: Curiosity

For years we noticed streaks on the lake:
Water currents? Wind ripples? Boat wakes?
Tide lines?! We laughed and scoffed
at each other's explanations, challenged them
with amateur-scientist expertise.

Google wasn't around to ask,
but when we met a noted limnologist,
he made short work of it:
Oily vegetative diatoms washing in
from the lake's perimeter.

Explanation is not always a relief.
Curiosity may kill the cat,
but thou shalt not kill the pleasure
of a dog gnawing on his bone.

Explanatory Value: Current Concerns

The historian and the fortune teller
wade in, holding hands,
preferring deep water to the shallows.

The structure of water
buoys and embraces them,
then buries them in the current.

Scientists deal with predictions,
the rest of us with guesses.
The future is enticing,

but present concerns
are the soil we dig, pondering
the puzzling, eternal sea.

Recycling

I

The robin takes off
with red wool yarn
combed from a Navaho rug by a snap,
woof from warp.

II

World War I army blankets shredded
back to wool, brightly dyed and woven,
were sold for a few bucks on Route 66
as Indian tribal souvenirs.

III

A Yankee farmhouse auction:
rugs good enough for a summer place,
their history shaken again and again,
made shorter by a thread or two.

IV

The nest coddles robin's-egg blue,
the red rewoven with birch bark and twigs,
a Native-inspired American basket
soon decomposed into native soil.

The Way Out

Spring's dusting of snow takes a frosty morning breath
and swallows cherry blossoms,
a disappearance one could only wish for.
Or is a fadeout better?
Plaudits to those who know how to leave:
the ballerina, radiant, off with a grand jeté.

September warms up
for October's technicolor strip show;
oak leaves are winter's party guests
who just don't get the hint.
Mud season says the snow has gone underground.

Crimson sumac candelabra light the way to summer
when we notice that we hadn't noticed
when they fell. I want to appreciate
the beauty of every loss. The space left
wants that space to leave you in.

The Effects of War

1.   Milkweed

It was like touching air,
soft, sensuous, slippery,
lighter than dandelions blown to the wind
or cattails exploding like silent sparklers.

I believed them when they said
it would save a downed pilot,
his lifejacket floating with a pound of its silk.
I'm even told it worked—and helped morale.

New to New England September color,
a child of World War II, I harvested happily.
I dreamed of being a war heroine:
twenty pounds of pods to save a life!

2.   Monarchs

Wings of stained glass,
they spend time sucking juice and leaves
of milkweed,
then journey three thousand miles
to arrive in kaleidoscopes
on Mexican firtree oyamel leaves.

3.   War

It's war out there—
in cornfields, meadows, and in Mexico.
Monarchs depend on milkweed,
juicy-good for poisoning predators.
Farmers poison weeds with pesticides;
milkweed is its victim.
The nurturing tropical forest is threatened
by tree-killing locals
and as usual the innocents are slaughtered.

Explanatory Value: The Writing on the Wall

The limits of language
delineate rocks where prayers of columbine
appear in Spring as miracles—
water-seeps the explanation.

Glyphs of the first snowfall
stutter on the rockface
like nascent poetry—
ledges, plates, cleavage planes—
and speak of geologic time,
the patience it takes
to develop a language without words.

Black Hole

The pond has taken in the night
      and given nothing back,
protecting itself from loss
with a thin, brittle skin.
      Go out in the dark
the first woolen-clouded winter night,
past the rise, beyond the reach
of streetlights.
Close your eyes and imagine
that when you open them,
stars will scatter in the grass, the moon
bounce like a ball. Follow its bounce
      and sing along,
let the black ice invite by cracking a smile,
welcoming you and the moon,
      Come in, come in.

Spring Cleaning

Harbingers of spring, you spiral
in a morning thermal you make tangible,
heading out to snack,
to clean the roads, the woods.
I salute your industry.

You muster air with a six-foot wingspan,
struggle to ride the rising tides,
fan out by day, congregate by night.
Your wings are more graceful than an eagle's;
angled in a slight *V,* you steady yourself
and tilt in static soaring flight.

You are many, swooping over my roof
as you return to your roost.
I welcome you to feed on death
without causing it. Why is it that
your very name is an epithet.

Someday Give a Day

Someday give a day,
go back and sit on the dock
in September, off season,
stepping into a diorama
where the wind has stopped working
and the light has lit the air and lake
alike. Your breath will seem an intrusion.

The glassy stillness will be beyond reflection.
This is where the heart goes to learn
to accept the settled look of death
and regrets the fish
that breaks the surface.

Notes and Dedications

"A Mind of Winter" owes much to Wallace Stevens.

"Explanatory Value: Naming" is written with Primo Levi in mind and dedicated to him.

"Safety in Numbers" is written for and about Giorgio Morandi.

"Orthophony: Listening" is based on a discovery of a teaching placard at the Norwich Historical Society. I tracked down the source, a happy discovery: *Orthophony; or The Cultivation of the Voice in Elocution.* William Russell, 1871, 39th edition.

"Touchstones" and "Minor Planet #2181" are dedicated to Eric Fogelin.

"We Teach Our Children How to Thank" is dedicated to John Fogelin.

"Starvation" is dedicated to my mother, "Help" to my mother and father, Florence and Irving Clay.

"Letter to Robert Frost." The winner of the Pick Your Favorite Poem Day was Rudyard Kipling's "If."

"Explanatory Value: Curiosity" is dedicated to Lars Fogelin.

"Explanatory Value: The Writing on the Wall" is dedicated to Rosamond Orford.

Thanks

The cover photograph is by Rosamond Orford (Upcountry Publishing, *Water Colours©*); her website is www.rosamond-orford.com. The author's photograph is by Alice Ritscherle. My warmest thanks to both of them.

I am grateful to April Ossmann, who consulted with expertise; to the Still Puddle Poets, Lampshade Poets, and Kendal Poets; and to Karen Kelsay of Kelsay Books and Delisa Hargrove, both of whom tolerated my less than adept handling of the computer programs.

My special thanks go to my sons, grandchildren, and daughters-in-law. And to Bob, whose presence clearly is in this book.

About the Author

Florence Fogelin's book, *Once It Stops* (Deerbrook Editions, 2015), was a finalist in Foreword Press's IndieFab Poetry Book of the Year 2016 competition. A chapbook, *Facing the Light,* was published in 2001.

Her poems have appeared in journals including *Prairie Schooner, Florida Review, Cumberland Poetry Review,* and *Poet Lore* and have been featured on websites by *Poetry Daily* and *Women's Voices for Change.* She has been a finalist for the Gell Prize by Writers & Books and semi-finalist for Word Work's Washington Prize.

Fogelin's poetry has appeared in anthologies including *53 Press Anthology 2013; Birchsong: Poetry Centered in Vermont; Roads Taken: Contemporary Vermont Poetry.* Fogelin was married to a professor of philosophy, Robert Fogelin (deceased), and has three adult sons. She currently lives in Hanover, NH, and has a website, florencefogelin.com.

www.ingramcontent.com/pod-product-compliance
Lightning Source LLC
Chambersburg PA
CBHW022016080426
42733CB00007B/624